REAL MONASTERIO DE SAN LORENZO DE EL ESCORIAL

Plan of the ground floor of the Monastery and the main floor of the King's Apartments
(*) areas not open to the public

The Palace of Philip II

THE KING'S APARTMENTS. Winter Palace

I THE COURTYARD OF MASKS
1 **THE QUEEN'S OR INFANTA'S QUARTERS**
   A) Queen's Staircase; B) Antechamber or Guardroom
The Queen's or Infanta's Chamber
   C) Main room; D) Bedroom; E) Study; F) Oratory
a) The Queen's Private Garden*

2 **THE KING'S QUARTERS**
   G) Hall of Portraits or Audience Room; H) Winter Walkway; I) Secretaries' Rooms*;
   J) Antechamber: King's Room; K) King's Staircase
The King's Chamber
   L) Main room; M) Bedroom; N) Study;
   O) Oratory
b) The King's Private Garden*

c) EL BOSQUECILLO*

THE PUBLIC PALACE

II ROYAL OR CARRIAGE COURTYARD. Gallery
Hall of Battles or Royal Gallery (*no. 27 in the partial plan of the main floor*)
3 Antechamber of Honour (*now the Museum of Painting*)
4 Hall of Honour or of St Maurice (*now the Museum of Painting*)
5 Ladies' Tower*
6 Former main staircase*
7 Ambassadors' apartments*
8 Lobby of main staircase by Villanueva
9 Dining room for Gentlemen of the Chamber (*now gift and book shop*)
d) Palace Garden*

ROYAL KITCHENS
III KITCHEN COURTYARD*
IV SERVANTS' OR PANTRY YARD*
10 Lobby of Royal Kitchen Staff (*now the entrance for general tours*)
11 Former Royal Kitchen (*now the ticket office*)
12 Former Royal Kitchen (*now the cafeteria*)

Around the Monastery
30 LA LONJA. Northern and western areas
31 FIRST CASA DE OFICIOS. Juan de Herrera
32 SECOND CASA DE OFICIOS. Juan de Herrera
33 HOUSE OF THE MINISTER OF STATE. Juan de Villanueva
34 INFANTES' HOUSE. Juan de Villanueva
35 CASA DE LA COMPAÑA. Francisco de Mora
36 Way down to the Casita del Príncipe and town of El Escorial
37 Way to the Casita del Infante

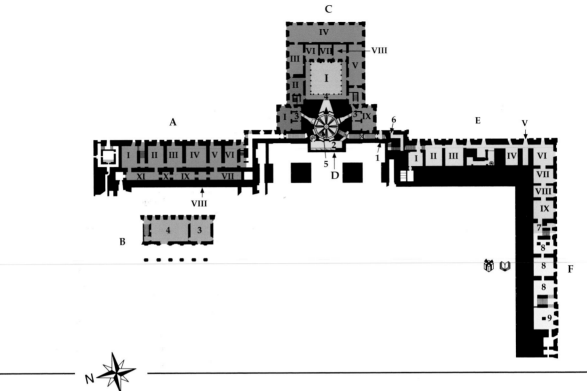

The Palace of the Bourbons

*(Restricted access, visits by appointment

II	PALACE OR COACH COURTYARD
III	KITCHEN COURTYARD*
IV	SERVANTS OR PANTRY COURTYARD*

THE KING'S QUARTERS

1. Main Staircase by Villanueva
2. Guard Rooms
3. Servants' Quarters. Former Main Staircase
4. King's Workshops
5. China Cabinet Room, formerly room leading to the Workshops
6. Gala Dining Room, formerly the Games
7. Dresser Room, vestibule by Villanueva's staircase
8. Ambassadors' Anteroom, formerly the Antechamber
9. Hall of Ambassadors, formerly the Courtroom
10. King's Oratory (Second Telemachus Room)
11. Audience Room, formerly the Dressing Room
12. Oval Room
13. Queen's Bedchamber, formerly a Study
14. **Fine Wood Rooms.** Ladies' Tower

A) Study; B) Ante-Oratory; C) Oratory D) Water closet

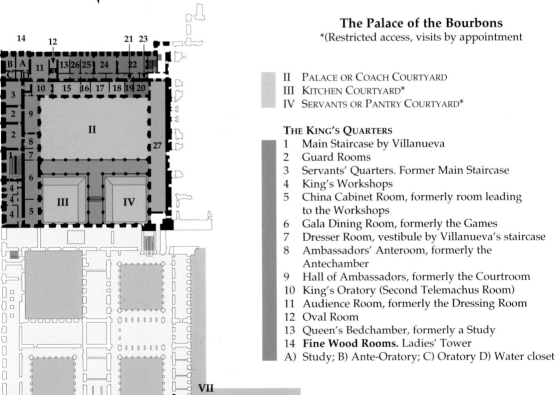

The New Museums

MUSEUM OF ARCHITECTURE

A VAULTS

Stairs leading down from the Hall of Honour (4)
Rooms I to VI: designs, drawings, prints and scale
models illustrating the Monastery's architectural
history
Rooms VII to XI: tools, materials, carpentry,
trades and models of machinery for the
construction of the Monastery

THE PANTHEONS

D KINGS' PANTHEON
1   Entrance and staircase
2   Rotting rooms*
3   Formerly corridors linking the King's
    and the Queen's Chambers in the
    Summer Palace to their galleries in the
    underground church*
4   Skylights in sepulchral chamber opening
    onto the Courtyard of Masks
5   Sepulchral chamber

E INFANTES' PANTHEON
6   Entrance stairs
Sepulchral chambers, from I to IX
7   Exit stairs leading up to the
Chapter Houses

F Gold and Silver Workshops

8   Cellars known as the Platerías, formerly the Monastery's silversmiths' workshops (*now gift and book shop*)
9   Room with experimental flat vault*. Juan Bautista de Toledo

MUSEUM OF PAINTING

B THE PUBLIC PALACE
3   Antechamber of Honour
4   Hall of Honour or of St Maurice

C THE KING'S APARTMENTS. Summer Palace
I COURTYARD OF MASKS
  Room I: Formerly the Queen's Summer
             Chamber Flemish school,
             16th century
  Room II: Flemish school, 17th century
  Room III: Italian school, 16th century
  Room IV: Formerly a Summer Walkway
             Paintings linked to Philip II's
             collection and to the High Altarpiece
             of the Basilica
  Room V: Italian school, 17th century
  Room VI: Spanish school, first half of the
             17th century
  Room VII: 17th-century Spanish school, Ribera
             and Zurbarán
  Room VIII: 17th-century Spanish school,
             high baroque
  Room IX: FORMERLY PHILIP II'S SUMMER
             CHAMBER
             Luca Giordano, Neapolitan baroque
             painter in the Royal Collections

THE INFANTA'S QUARTERS
15 Telemachus Room, formerly the Recreation Room
16 King's Room, formerly the Bedchamber
17 Pompeian Drawing Room, formerly the
    Wet Nurses' Room
18 Entrance hall

THE QUEEN'S QUARTERS
19 Usher's Room
20 Anteroom leading to the Hall of Battles
21 Passage Room
22 Courtroom
23 Queen's Oratory
24 Private Dining Room, formerly the Boudoir
25 Bedchamber, now called that of the King
26 Water Closet

The Palace of Philip II
THE PUBLIC PALACE
27 Hall of Battles or Royal Gallery

The Royal Library of St Lawrence
VII KINGS' COURTYARD
28 Entrance stairs
29 Main Hall or Print Room
30 Exit stairs

REAL MONASTERIO DE SAN LORENZO DE EL ESCORIAL

CARMEN GARCÍA-FRÍAS
JOSÉ LUIS SANCHO

R✦S
REALES SITIOS DE ESPAÑA

© PATRIMONIO NACIONAL, 2007
Palacio Real de Madrid
Bailén, s/n
28071 Madrid
Tel. 91 547 53 50

© Texts: Carmen García-Frías and
José Luis Sancho Gaspar

© Photographs: Patrimonio Nacional - Félix Lorrio
Aldeasa - José Barea

NIPO: 006-07-021-5
ISBN: 978-84-7120-355-7 (1.ªed., 3.ªimp.)
National book catalogue number: M-33400-2007

Co-ordination and production: ALDEASA
Design and layout: Myriam López Consalvi
Photograph setting: Lucam
Printed: Artes Gráficas Palermo, S.L.

Cover photograph: A view of the Monastery as seen from
Monte Abantos.

Back cover photograph: Monastery pastureland.

Printed in Spain

Contents

Foreword

PATRIMONIO NACIONAL is the institution which administers the State properties in the service of the Crown by performing the representative functions assigned to it by the Spanish Constitution and Spanish law.

These properties comprise a number of palaces, monasteries and convents founded by monarchs, which are of great historic, artistic and cultural importance; most significantly, they are of outstanding symbolic value. The Royal Palaces of Madrid, El Pardo, Aranjuez, San Ildefonso and La Almudaina continue to be used for the residential and representative purposes for which they were built centuries ago. In these buildings His Majesty the King carries out his duties as Head of State – particularly in the Royal Palace of Madrid, which is the official royal residence and, as such, the highest embodiment of this symbolic value.

In addition to these functions, Patrimonio Nacional has a specific cultural duty consisting of making the buildings and other possessions available for study and research and visits by the public.

Both the buildings and the Spanish Royal Collections (comprising 27 different categories ranging from fans to tools and including silverware, painting, tapestries, furniture, musical instruments and clocks, etc.) are distinguished by the very characteristics that make Patrimonio Nacional a unique cultural institution. These are: *their particular purpose*, since they are still used by the Spanish royal family; their *historical authenticity*, as the items were once commissioned, acquired or presented as gifts for the buildings that house them; their *originality*, given the absence of replicas or imitations; and their extraordinary *artistic, historic and symbolic value*. The visitor will therefore appreciate that Patrimonio Nacional is much more than just a museum.

The Spanish Royal Palaces are surrounded by green spaces that currently span approximately 20,500 hectares. Gardens and parkland account for some 500 and the remaining 20,000 is woodland (parts of which are open to the public) belonging to El Pardo, La Herrera and Riofrío. These areas, mainly of the *Mediterranean forest* biotype, are of great ecological importance and provide a worthy setting for the monuments they surround.

Since their foundation, the Royal Monasteries and Convents have been served by the same religious orders, except for San Lorenzo de El Escorial, which passed from the Hieronymites to the Augustinians as a result of disentailment in the 19th century. They enjoy special importance in Spanish history, as they owe their establishment to the personal patronage of the monarchs.

In addition to serving a cultural purpose, the tours organised for the general public attempt to make Spanish visitors more fully aware of the symbolic value of these places, so that they may identify with them and feel they are heirs to Patrimonio Nacional's immense historical and artistic treasures.

The influence of these treasures, acquired by the Spanish Crown over the centuries, on Spain's cultural identity has been, and continues to be, decisive.

Introduction

The Monastery of El Escorial is the monument which best represents the ideological and cultural aspirations of the Spanish Golden Age. During this era, the Spanish Crown, which had established itself as the main defender of the Catholic Counter-Reformation while other countries had embraced the Protestant Reform movement, became the leading world power on account of its dynastic alliances and resulting territorial power in Europe, and by gaining control of practically the whole of the recently discovered continent of America.

The "Catholic" king's struggle for European hegemony, the defence of the traditional religion and the cult of the dynasty and of the monarch as God's chosen one, find expression in El Escorial through an original combination of Italian and Flemish artistic forms.

El Escorial remains under the royal patronage of H.M. the king to this day and is administered by Patrimonio Nacional. Before commencing our tour of the monument, it is worth examining its historical background.

General background

The reasons for the foundation

THE BUILDING at San Lorenzo el Real serves a variety of purposes, though it was originally designed as a monastery for the monks of the order of St Jerome. Its church was the pantheon of Emperor Charles V and his wife, and of their son Philip II and relatives and heirs, where the monks prayed endlessly for the salvation of the royal family. A palace to house the king – the patron of the foundation – and his entourage was also designed. The school and seminary complete the Monastery's religious function, while the Library provides a service to all three centres.

The victory over Henry II of France at Saint Quentin, the first major conquest of Philip II's reign, coincided with St Lawrence's feast day on 10 August 1557. This partly explains why the Monastery, which is not merely a monument of worship, was dedicated to this saint.

Charles V also played a decisive part in the Monastery's foundation given his enormous spiritual influence over his son; he had set an example by spending his last years among the Hieronymite monks of Yuste and needed to be given a worthy burial.

The founder

PHILIP II became king of Spain and of the Indies in 1556, king of Naples, Sicily and Milan in 1554 and king of the Netherlands a year later as his father, Emperor Charles V, progressively stepped down from power and finally, in 1556, retired to the Monastery of Yuste, where he died in 1558. Philip II died at El Escorial on 13 September 1598.

The construction

HAVING DECIDED to build the Monastery, Philip II began his search for the ideal site in 1558, which he finally located in 1562. Work began on the project or "universal design" by Juan Bautista de Toledo. By 1571 the Monastery area was almost complete and work commenced on the so-called "King's Apartments" in 1572 and on the Basilica in 1574. The Basilica was consecrated in 1595, the year the works can be considered to have reached completion, though the last stone was in fact laid in 1584, and the task of decoration dragged on for several more years.

◀ *Palace Garden.*

The king personally supervised the whole construction process, responsibility for which fell to the architect, the prior and two committees.

The architect was directly appointed by the king. As such, he only answered to Philip II rather than to the prior, who was otherwise the main person responsible for the works and headed the "Congregation", the executive committee in charge of legal and financial affairs, inspections and payments.

The architects

EL ESCORIAL can by no means be considered the work of a single architect; rather, it is the product of close collaboration between two men – Juan Bautista de Toledo and Juan de Herrera. Juan Bautista de Toledo, who had worked under Michelangelo in the Vatican, was entrusted with the general site plan and most of the design drawings. During the period when Juan de Herrera was in charge of the works, the construction of practically all of the complex was completed, including many parts that had not been designed by Toledo. If we take into account the many contributions made by other Spanish and Italian architects, then the final result of El Escorial should be regarded as a highly personal manifestation of Philip II's character.

Nor should we forget the important role of the master builders and overseers, such as Brother Antonio de Villacastin, Pedro de Tolosa, Diego de Alcantara and Juan de Minjares. Francisco de Mora was a disciple of Herrera who continued this architect's work from 1583 onwards. And in the 18th century, the major works carried out for Charles II and Charles IV by Juan de Villanueva, who had received a classical training in Italy, were imbued with the spirit of El Escorial.

General view of the Monastery from the Casita del Infante. ▲

▲ *Above, Monastery roofs. Below, Main entrance to the Monastery.*

THE MONASTERY was run in accordance with its founder's wishes and intentions until 1835, and was enriched with the contributions made by the succeeding monarchs.

Philip III began work on the *Kings' Pantheon*. Philip IV completed it and procured a significant collection of paintings, entrusting Velázquez with the task of selecting and arranging them in 1656. Following a fire in 1671, Charles II had Bartolomé Zumbigo rebuild the Monastery and adorn the Sacristy with an *altarpiece* incorporating Claudio Coello's *Adoration of the Blessed Sacrament* and with a series of grandiose frescoes by Luca Giordano. In 1767 Charles III gave orders for the Royal Seat of San Lorenzo de El Escorial to be developed and new houses were built around La Lonja in addition to the Casita del Príncipe and the Casita del Infante, recreational lodges for the prince and his brother, respectively. Charles IV had the northern façade remodelled and the Palace of the Bourbons decorated, as well as enriching the decoration of the Casita built for him when he was still Prince.

El Escorial in the 19th and 20th centuries

Following the depletion of the El Escorial art collection during the War of Independence, which was partially compensated for by the works returned and restored by Ferdinand VII, the community of Hieronymite monks was forced by the disentailment laws of the 19th century to abandon the Monastery and its assets became Crown property. The Monastery was then used for various religious purposes until it was finally granted to the Augustinian monks in 1885. The Fourth Centenary celebrations commemorating the beginning of the construction in 1963 and its completion in

View of the King's Gardens from a balcony. ▶

1986 gave fresh impetus to restoration work and to studies on El Escorial, which seem to have superseded earlier positive or negative evaluations distorted by prejudice.

The tour

THE ROYAL Monastery of San Lorenzo de El Escorial consists of a huge rectangle that houses the building's various functions, as the plan illustrates:

The holy area comprising the Church and its atrium.

The Monastery, laid out around one large and four small courtyards.

The King's Apartments.

The outbuildings of the King's Palace.

The School.

The Library.

This "universal design" devised by Juan Bautista de Toledo is influenced by the cross-shaped floor plans of 15th-century Italian and Spanish hospitals, but its main source of inspiration can be regarded as the traditional layout of medieval monasteries. The Monastery is located on a mountain slope, with its façades oriented towards the four cardinal directions and the altar facing eastwards in such a way that on this and the southern side, where the land slopes down, it is enclosed by gardens supported by thick walls. The northern and western sides, where the terrain is higher, are surrounded by an open area called *La Lonja*.

As the ascent comes to an end, the most picturesque aspect of the building comes into sight, with the King's Apartments, the rear of the Basilica and its dome. The *main façade* is reached by crossing La Lonja and encircling the whole building. The Monastery is impressive for its uniformity and lack of ornamentation, though each façade has its own individual character.

◀ *On the previous page, general view of the Monastery at night.*

View of the south facade of the Monastery, showing the Gallery of Convalescents and the orchard pond. ▲

Juan Bautista de Toledo did not originally intend the building to be so uniform. His design featured one less floor in the western section of the building and towers, marking the transition to a greater height in the centres of the northern and southern façades. Staggered floors would have given the building a harmonious appearance more in keeping with high Renaissance style. In 1564, Philip II decided to increase the number of monks in the Monastery from fifty to one hundred, and the design was accordingly adapted to incorporate four floors to the whole of the building. Visitors' access is through the door in the centre of the *northern façade*, where entrance tickets can be purchased. After buying a ticket, it is a good idea to go out again and head for the main doorway, as the northern façade and buildings surrounding La Lonja were constructed between the 16th and 17th centuries as outbuildings of the Palace and Monastery and were not envisaged in Juan Bautista de Toledo's initial design.

The two *Casas de Oficios* or Servants' Houses are located opposite the northern façade, which was remodelled in the 18th century by Juan de Villanueva. These houses were built by Juan de Herrera in the 16th century to accommodate the king's servants, and were later linked to the Palace in 1769 by an *underground passage* built by Father Pontones (Friar Antonio de San José) to prevent the royal attendants' wigs and three-cornered hats being blown off by the strong winds. The *Casa de la Compaña*, which stands at the southwesternmost end of La Lonja and was built at the end of the 16th century by Francisco de Mora as monastery facilities, is linked to the Monastery by a gallery supported by arches.

Up until Charles III's reign, there were no buildings of any significance around the Monastery: the main façade looked out on the mountain, establishing a contrast between Nature and Art. The Hieronymite monks lived like hermits and devoted their time to prayer in the midst of the wilderness.

The other buildings that surround La Lonja were thus designed by Juan de Villanueva in the 18th century. Next to the Casa de la Compaña stand the long *Infantes' House*, begun in 1771, and, at an angle to it, the *House of the Minister of State*, which dates from 1785. Both have splendid staircases.

The main façade of the Monastery has three doorways. The side doors, identical in design, give access to the School (on the left) and the Monastery (on the right).

The doorway to the Monastery is not its main entrance; it led by way of a ramp to the food stores. Behind it is the impressive *kitchen* and remarkable *skylight-roofed* courtyard located between the four lesser cloisters. The layout is more or less similar to that of the School, which boasts a main hall or "theatre".

The *main doorway*, located in the centre of this façade, leads to the Monastery and Basilica and is therefore of religious significance. Its design does not bear any relation to the building onto which it is built – the library – but rather to the church, whose real façade is located at the far end of the atrium.

Herrera actually drew inspiration for this doorway from an engraving by Serlio of a church façade; Philip II, himself no newcomer to architectural treatises, may well have been aware of this source. The royal coat-of-arms and the St Lawrence were created by Juan Bautista Monegro.

The *vestibule*, above which the Library lies, leads to the *Kings' Courtyard*, which is overlooked by the large *dome* and the *façade of the Basilica*.

The *sculptures* of the six great kings of Judea that adorn the upper section of the façade were also fashioned by Juan Bautista Monegro, like the St Lawrence. All seven figures were

Presbytery of the Basilica, showing the High Altarpiece. ▶

sculpted from the same block of granite which came from a quarry in the mountains, on which the following inscription was carved: "six kings and a saint / emerged from this rock / and there was still room for more." The courtyard was originally designed by Juan Bautista de Toledo with side porticos, but these were never built. The right-hand tower is the clock or bell tower; the one on the left was named the tower "of the chimes" after a Flemish organ, which was re-installed in 1988.

On climbing the steps to the *Basilica portico*, we come across an entrance in the right-hand wall. This used to be the main entrance to the Monastery, and we will leave through this doorway after completing our visit.

The Basilica

THIS GREAT monastic church is the true raison d'être of El Escorial. Although Juan Bautista de Toledo established its location and boundaries in his "universal design", the end result was not his project alone but rather a combined effort incorporating a variety of ideas under the influence of Juan de Herrera.

Juan Bautista de Toledo's design included a semi-circular apse flanked by towers; in 1562 the engineer-architect Francesco Paciotto strongly criticised its overall proportions and came up with a square-shaped design in 1563. Toledo produced another design in 1567 and, from this year on until 1572, Philip II had the best Italian architects present designs, which were examined, along with the Spanish projects, by the Florentine Academy and by Vignola in Rome. After studying all the designs in 1573, Philip II decided they were not what he was looking for and, after further hesitation, it seems that Herrera's project, based on Paciotti's ideas, was finally chosen in 1574. The end result is similar to the Genoese church of Santa Maria di Carignano. The organisational skills of Juan de Herrera and the master builder, Brother Antonio de Villacastin, shone in the construction work.

The Basilica actually consists of two churches: the one used by the general public, located *under the choir*, and the Royal Chapel and monastery church, which make up the main body.

The ground plan of the public church is a smaller scale copy of the main church. Its central section is covered by a rather boldly designed *flat vault*. Two altars on either side of the central arch were used for giving mass to the townspeople. Located between this area and the Royal Chapel is the *Seminarians' Choir*, which is separated from the chapel by large bronze railings cast by Guillén de Tujarón in Saragossa.

Above the public church, at first-floor level, is the *Monks' Choir*, which is closed to the public; the stalls were carved by José Flecha, a Genoese, and the organ cases were fashioned by Enrique Cotén. One of the 124 stalls, located in the southwest corner, is slightly wider than the others: Philip II sat there when listening to services in the Choir area. The fresco on the vault, *The Glory*, was painted by Luca Cambiaso, known in Spain as *Luqueto*.

Several of the human figures are portraits, including those of the artist himself and of Brother Antonio de Villacastín. The paintings on the walls, which remained unfinished at his death, were completed by Romulo Cincinnato.

Before going past the bronze railings, the visitor's attention is drawn to the *Main Chapel*, with its enormous *high altarpiece* at the far end and the royal cenotaphs at the sides, according to a classical design by Juan de Herrera. All the gilt bronze sculpture work is by the two Milanese artists, Leone and Pompeo Leoni.

The delightful *Tabernacle* in the lower section was designed by Herrera and built between 1579 and 1586 by Jacome da Trezzo

Above left, general view of the Basilica crossing and on the right, view of the Basilica vaults and dome. ▶
Below, the Choir.

using a variety of different Spanish marbles. The two canvases adorning the first floor of the Basilica and the one in the centre of the second floor were painted by Pellegrino Tibaldi. The rest are by Federico Zuccaro.

The cenotaphs of Charles V on the Gospel side (left) and of Philip II on the Epistle side (right) are crowned by their respective coat-of-arms. There are three doors situated below the cenotaphs: the one nearest the pulpit leads to the Sacristy and Relics Chapel, and the other two lead onto the small *oratories* next to the King's and Queen's bedrooms.

This arrangement is based on the Emperor's quarters in Yuste. It might also be said that in this way Philip II practically slept over his father's tomb, and prayed beneath the place appointed for his own burial effigy showing him in prayer. Philip II is surrounded by his wives: Elizabeth of Valois, Mary of Portugal (the mother of Prince Charles who is at her side) and Anne of Austria. Opposite them, next to an armed Charles V wearing the imperial mantle, is the Empress Isabella (Philip II's mother) and, behind her, her daughter Maria, followed by the emperor's sisters, Mary of Hungary and Eleanor of France.

The *Presbytery vault* is decorated, like that of the choir, with frescoes by Luqueto depicting the *Coronation of the Virgin*. The remaining *vaults* were coated with stucco in the 16th century, and in 1693 Charles II commissioned Luca Giordano to decorate them with frescoes, creating an impressive baroque appearance.

Giordano is well known in Spain as Lucas Jordán on account of the many works he executed for and in this country. Because of his skill and speed, he was assigned great quantities

▲ *On the left, Cenotaph of Philip II. On the right, tomb sculpture of Charles V and his family by Leoni.*

Sculpture of Philip II and his family in prayer by Leoni (detail). ▶

EXTRVXIT SIBI VIVENS P
QVIESCVNT SIMVL ANNA
LISABETHA ET MARIA VXOR
VM CAROLO PRINC . FIL . PRIM

of work and was appropriately nicknamed "Fa presto" or "speedy". Giordano painted these vaults and the one above the Monastery staircase in only 22 months, from September 1692 to July 1694, when he was 57 years old.

In addition to the large reliquary-altars painted by Federico Zuccaro, which are situated at the head of the two side aisles (The *Annunciation* and *St Jerome in the Desert*) there are another forty altarpieces (thirty-six in the church, and two in the area under the choir) adorned with canvases distributed around the various chapels and recesses of the Basilica, which are the work of Spanish artists Juan Fernández de Navarrete "the Mute", Luis de Carvajal, Diego de Urbina and Alonso Sanchez Coello, and Italian artists Luca Cambiaso, Romulo Cincinnato and Pellegrino Tibaldi.

The decoration of the Basilica is completed by the two large bronze *Tenebrae* and *carnation* candelabras, fashioned by Juan Simon de Amberes, around 1571; and the two *pulpits* by Manuel de Urquiza, commissioned by Ferdinand VII around 1830.

A masterpiece of 16th-century Italian sculpture is exhibited in one of the chapels at the foot of the church: the superb *Christ on the Cross* in Carrara marble which Benvenuto Cellini sculpted between 1559 and 1562 for his own tomb in the Florentine church of the Santissima Annunziata. It never occupied this place because the Grand Duke of Tuscany persuaded him to sell it to him, and he later gave it to Philip II. Engraved with the author's name and date on the pedestal, this nude sculpture has an admirable morbid beauty.

▲ *Luca Giordano: vault decorated with a fresco painting of the Exodus of the Israelites.*

Top, general view of the Kings' Courtyard, showing the Basilica facade. ▲
Bottom left, Benvenuto Cellini: Christ on the Cross, *and right, Façade of the Library overlooking the Kings' Courtyard .*

▲ *Pellegrino Tibaldi. Frescoes on the vault, 1586-91. Library, Main Hall or Hall of Honour.*

On leaving the Basilica, we once again cross the Kings' Courtyard and climb a staircase on the right of vestibule to the *Library*, pausing for a moment to contemplate the stark beauty of the façade that looks onto the Kings' Courtyard.

The Library

THE ORIGINAL design of the Monastery envisaged the Library merely as one of the rooms surrounding the Cloister and it did not gain its current special and symbolic significance until much later. It provides a link between the Monastery and School (it is used by both), and acts as a sort of threshold to the central axis of the building, and therefore combines knowledge, faith and power. Both its location and the richness of its decoration evidence the importance Philip II attached to the Library within the complex.

The visit comprises the *Main Hall* or Hall of Honour, which contains printed books, though there was also a room for manuscripts and another where prohibited printed matter and books were kept. The significance that Philip II attached to the Library is consonant with the importance he afforded the Seminary and the School from 1579 onwards, inspired by the spirit of the Council of Trent. But it is also due in part to the prestige that a Royal Library lent the Spanish Crown – a library which could be regarded as the accumulation of knowledge and a "precious reserve" of original codices.

Although the collection has been badly depleted on several occasions, the worst being the fire in 1671, the Library still houses over 40,000 works, including an impressive number of Latin, Greek, Arabic and Hebrew manuscripts.

In addition to its own holdings, which numbered over 4,000 volumes, and the books

General view of the Library. ▶

and manuscripts belonging to the Crown that had previously been kept in the Royal Chapel of Granada, the king had several private collections brought to El Escorial. Father Sigüenza and Benito Arias Montano were entrusted with the task of sorting and classifying this huge collection, to which 4,000 Arabic manuscripts were incorporated during the reign of Philip III.

Given its many windows – seven of which open onto the Kings' Courtyard and five onto La Lonja – the Main Hall of the Library, which measures 55 metres long and 10 metres wide, is "bright, full of majesty and light". Its shelves and frescoes are an impressive sight. The frescoes, painted between 1586 and 1593 by Pellegrino Tibaldi in mannerist style, are clearly influenced by Michelangelo. The complex and extensive iconographic scheme, which mostly

depicts sages and prominent men of antiquity, was designed by the chronicler of El Escorial's foundation, Brother Jose de Sigüenza.

The series of frescoes by Tibaldi begins on the School side, where the entrance is, with a representation of *Philosophy*, and, on the south or Monastery side, with a representation of *Theology*. In between them are the sciences, or the seven liberal arts, according to the medieval dictums of the Trivium (Grammar, Rhetoric and Dialectics) and the Quadrivium (Arithmetic, Music, Geometry and Astrology). There is an allegoric representation of one of these arts in each section of the vault; they are flanked on either side, in the semicircular areas or lunettes, by two learned disciples of the science in question. The friezes beneath the cornice are adorned with further references to the science.

▲ *Detail of the fresco painting in the Library vault, by Pellegrino Tibaldi.*

Detail of one of the Library shelves. ▲

The monumental *Doric bookcases* were built by José Flecha, Juan Senén and Martín de Gamboa according to a design by Juan de Herrera. The books are placed with the leaves facing outwards to allow the paper to "breathe". Their gilt edges are visible through the 18th-century metal meshing and "the room thus looks beautiful as it is painted or covered in gold from bottom to top".

The shelves, mounted on marble bases, are carved from wood from the New World. The column shafts are made of beefwood and the base and capitals of orange wood. The five brown marble tables that are distributed throughout the hall date from the time of the Monastery's foundation, while the two octagonal porphyry ones were made by the marble cutter Bartolomé Zumbigo around 1660. All of the aforementioned tables display a large collection of world and celestial globes, maps, astrolabes and other items, indicating the Library's status of cabinet of science. This is further borne out by the armillary sphere built by Antonio Santucci around 1582, in accordance with the Ptolemaic system, the world and celestial spheres made by Jean Blaeu in approximately 1660 and the magnet stone that was apparently found during the excavations to lay the foundations.

Other noteworthy examples of cabinetwork include the 18th-century *cupboard* which is inlaid with ebony and boxwood and contains the Library's coin collection. Also of interest is the baroque *doorway* built in 1622 leading out into the Guests' Courtyard. Descending the Guests' Staircase beside the doorway we come to the Kings' Courtyard, where the tour of the Museums begins.

The Museums

HAVING RETURNED to the King's Courtyard after coming down from the Library, we leave the

Top, building and masonry tools. Bottom, model of one of the spires of the towers. ▲

El Greco: The Martyrdom of Saint Maurice and the Theban Legion. ▲

building and re-enter it through the main doorway in the northern façade, where the entrance tickets are purchased. This doorway once led directly to the Palace kitchens, now converted into ticket offices and a cafeteria. Through these, or through the vestibule, we enter the *Palace* or *Carriage Courtyard*, whose eastern and southern walkways are decorated with two series depicting battles fought in Philip II's reign. The one by the 17th-century Flemish school shows scenes from the Netherlands campaign, and the other one, by Luca Cambiaso, depicts the Battle of Lepanto.

It is only possible to appreciate its full size from the main floor as half of it is taken up by a T-shaped two-storey block that was formerly the *royal kitchen* premises. The rest rooms are now located here.

The rooms to the east and north of the Palace Courtyard form the *Palace of the Bourbons*. During the Habsburg rule, the northern rooms were occupied by the ladies and gentlemen of the court, and the eastern rooms were used by the king's children.

New Museums

The eastern gallery of the Palace Courtyard leads to the exhibition space formed by the Museum of Architecture and the Museum of Painting via two rooms that belonged to the 16th-century Public Palace or Administrative Palace. The first houses the polychrome woodcarving of *St Michael Triumphs over Lucifer,* by Luisa Roldán, "La Roldana", court sculptor to Charles II. The second displays the superb painting by Domenikos Theotokopoulos, *The Martyrdom of St Maurice and the Theban Legion,* which Philip II commissioned for the Basilica. However, the work was not to the king's liking for reasons of "decorum", as the iconographic representation did not conform

▲ *Models of the cranes used to construct the Monastery.*

to Counter-Reformation standards, and it was eventually replaced by a painting by Romulo Cincinnato. The walls of both rooms are also hung with various Flemish tapestries from Philip II's collection, the most outstanding of which are the famous *Triumph of the Mother of God series*, known as the *Paños de Oro*.

Museum of Architecture

A staircase located behind the El Greco painting leads down to these rooms, which were opened in 1963 and enhanced after the exhibitions held there in 1986. They house plans, scale-models and other objects arranged didactically to illustrate the construction process of the building.

Museum of Painting

The ground-floor rooms of the *King's Apartments*, the so-called *Summer Palace*, were renovated in 1963 to house the works from the Monastery picture collection that were not

On the left, Paolo Cagliari, known as Veronese: the Annunciation, ▲
and on the right, Juan Fernández de Navarrete, the Mute: the Beheading of St James.

transferred to the Museo del Prado in the 19th and 20th centuries. The first room now holds the 16th-century Flemish paintings, particularly works by Michel Coxcie, one of Philip II's favourite painters whose style shows the Italian influence of Raphael and Leonardo. Fine examples are the *Christ Carrying the Cross, David and Goliath,* and the *St Philip Tryptich,* a tribute to the king's patron saint.

17th-century Flemish paintings are on display in the second room. *Philip III Passing through San Sebastián,* depicting a moment prior to the signing of the marriage agreements between the Spanish and French monarchies and attributed to Paul van der Muelen, hangs in pride of place. Beside it are a *Country Landscape* by Jan Brueghel II the Younger and two *Vases* by Daniel Seghers, among others.

The third room is devoted to 16th-century Italian painting, mainly the Venetian school, examples of which are Titian's *St Margaret,* the *God the Father and the Holy Ghost* attributed to Paolo Veronese, and two *Descents,* one by Veronese and the other by his son Carlo. The other works include a magnificent *St Michael* by Luca Cambiaso.

The fourth room houses a masterpiece by Roger van der Weyden, the *Calvary,* and various late-16th-century Italian and Spanish canvases closely linked to the Monastery's origins, such as Veronese's *Annunciation,* Tintoretto's *Adoration of the Shepherds,* and the *Nativity* and *Epiphany* that were commissioned from Federico Zucarro for the high altar of the Basilica but never hung there. The room also contains major works by Juan Fernández de Navarrete, "the Mute", such as *St Jerome in Penitence* and the *Beheading of St James,* among others.

The fifth room displays 17th-century Italian works. Particularly noteworthy are the interesting portrait of *Innocent X with a Prelate,* by Pietro Martire Neri, four works by Guercino

and two – *St Augustine* and *St Monica* – by Guido Reni.

The three inner rooms (the sixth, seventh and ninth), which look onto the Courtyard of Masks, contain 17th-century Spanish works. The sixth brings together those executed in the first half of the century, including two *Still Lifes with Goldfinches* by Juan van der Hamen, and the *Nativity of the Virgin* by Jusepe Leonardo. The seventh is devoted to Ribera and Zurburán, including works by their followers and studio replicas. The *Apparition of the Christ Child to St Anthony* is attributed to Ribera and the *Presentation of the Virgin in the Temple* to Zurburán, though other historians believe both to be mainly studio works. The collection of the work of the Spanish school continues into the eighth room, which contains high-Baroque artists such as Claudio Coello, who painted the *Portrait of Mariana of Austria;* the attribution of the *Portrait of Mariana of Neuberg* is more doubtful. It also contains Alonso Cano's *Virgin and Sleeping Child* and Francisco Rizzi's *Annunciation.*

The ninth and last room, formerly Philip II's summer bedchamber (linked to the gallery of the "underground church" that he used as an oratory and is now the Kings' Pantheon) is devoted to the work of Luca Giordano, who worked actively for the Monastery in the late 17th century. The Monastery houses many of his frescoes and a considerable number of canvases, which are mostly religious except for the *Portrait of Charles II* shown in this room.

The tour of the Museum of Painting ends here. A corridor leads out into the Courtyard of Masks.

Courtyard of Masks

THIS COURTYARD, which is overshadowed by the enormous façade of the Church, owes its name

to the two fountains in its eastern wall; the rest of the yard is surrounded by porticos formed by semicircular arches resting on Tuscan columns – a style appropriate to a country residence. The roofs and curious chimney tops add a Flemish note to the obviously Italian-style design of this courtyard. The only elements left untouched by the terrible fire of 1671 were the roofs of this part of the building, the *King's Apartments,* built around the yard on two floors, with the summer rooms (as we have seen) on the ground floor and the winter rooms on the main floor, as we are about to see.

The King's Apartments

THE KING'S Apartments are symbolically located along the central axis of the building, and are closely linked to the holy area. This arrangement would appear to underline the role of the king,

protected by Divine Grace, as defender of the Faith, mediator between the sacred and the profane (Monastery and Palace), but at the same time separated from mere mortals by these rooms which "no-one can enter without permission, like eagles in their eyries". Despite their modest size and appearance, the King's Apartments are the focal point of the whole complex, since from here the monarch had access to all parts of the Monastery.

Like all the palaces of the Spanish monarchs of that time, these small apartments at El Escorial were divided into two similarly laid-out *quarters* for both the *King* and the *Queen.* They were designed in such a way that the Church's high altar could be seen from their respective bedchambers through the adjoining Oratory "so that the monarchs are inside (so to speak) and yet outside the main chapel; such a design could not be greater or

▲ *The Courtyard of Masks.*

General view of the Gallery of Battles. Fresco paintings by Granello, Castello, Cambiaso and Tavarone. ▶

more dignified". The queen's quarters are attributed the highest honour of being located on the Gospel side (on the left, if one faces the altar); after the king was widowed for the fourth and last time in 1580, the Queen's rooms were used by her daughter, Isabella Clara Eugenia, which is why they are usually called the *Infanta's Quarters*. Ascending the Queen's staircase from the Courtyard of Masks we come to the *Queen's* or the *Infanta's Quarters*, but it is also possible to come out into the last room of the "Public Palace" adjoining the King's Apartments: The Gallery of Battles.

The *Gallery of Battles*, a huge room 55 metres long, is covered in frescoes depicting war scenes (hence the name) painted by Fabrizio Castello, Orazio Cambiaso and Lazzaro Tavarone. These "long rooms", as they were known, were typical of that period and were used as covered walkways as well as for solemn receptions.

Philip II wished to demonstrate the connection between his campaigns for European hegemony and the combative attitude of the Spanish Christian monarchs of the Middle Ages. The *Battle of La Higueruela*, John II of Castile's victory over the natives of Granada in 1431, painted on the long wall facing the windows (it is a copy of a long 15th-century sketch found in the Alcázar palace in Segovia) thus contrasts with war scenes that took place during Philip II's reign. These scenes, painted above and between the balconies, consist of nine episodes of Philip II's war against France, including a painting of the famous Battle of San Quentin, and two scenes from the sea battles for the Portuguese crown fought off the Azores.

▲ *On the left, detail of the fresco painting of the Battle of La Higueruela in the Gallery of Battles and, on the right, general view of the Hall of Portraits.*

Entering the Queen's or Infanta's Quarters we come to the *Antechamber*, which in turn leads into the *Chamber* or *Bedroom of the Infanta*. The presbytery of the church can be seen from this chamber and the windows look out onto the *Queen's Garden*.

The portrait of *Isabella Clara Eugenia* by Bartolomé González hangs next to that of her sister, Catherine Michaela, by the school of Sánchez Coello. The small hand organ dates from the 16th century and bears Philip II's coat-of-arms on its front.

We return to the *Antechamber* via the corridors on the upper floor of the Courtyard of Masks which link the King's Bedchamber with that of the queen. This Antechamber is decorated with various paintings by Juan Correa de Vivar and from the Bassanos' studio. *Philip II's sedan chair* is also found in this chamber.

The chair, which was used by the gout-ridden king in the last years of his life, incorporates a curious system for reclining the back. The structure enabled a canopy to be placed on top and the sides closed off.

We next come to the *King's Quarters*. The arrangement and use of the rooms of Spanish royal palaces were governed by the Burgundian etiquette, imposed by Charles V, which reinforced the "sacred" identity of the monarch: access to each room was increasingly more restricted, depending on the visitor's rank. The Talavera tiled frieze covering the lower part of the walls is original. In general, the furnishing of these rooms is in keeping with what they were known to contain in the 16th century.

The Antechamber leads to the *Audience Room*, now known as the Hall of Portraits after the likenesses of the members of the House of

Infanta's Chamber. ▲ 41

Austria that hang there. These portraits were painted by Sir Anthony More, Sánchez Coello, Pantoja de la Cruz and Juan Carreño de Miranda.

This room was used for ordinary audiences granted by the King. The Chinese folding chairs from the Ming era (second half of the 16th century) were used by the king to rest his gouty leg. Among the most noteworthy of the paintings is Sir Anthony More's portrait of Philip II aged 35 and dressed in the armour of the *Battle of Saint Quentin*.

The Hall of Portraits leads to the *Walkway*, which in turn leads to the King's Room through two wooden inlaid doors, "of the best and most masterfully carved to come to us from Germany, expertly designed and understood", that Emperor Maximilian II sent Philip II in 1567 as a gift. The Walkway, located inside the King's Quarters, was a typical feature of 16th-century European palaces and was used for indoor strolls when the weather was bad.

The arrangement of the canvases depicting military actions from the reign of Philip II (there were formerly Flemish landscapes) and engravings of maps by the famous 16th-century geographer Abraham Ortelius is more or less in line with Father Sigüenza's descriptions. The *meridians* on the floor of this room and the following one are the work of the Jesuit Johannes Wedlingen (1755).

The two inward facing rooms looking out onto the Courtyard of Masks, which lie parallel to this walkway and can be seen from its doors, are decorated with paintings from the 16th and 17th centuries. The most noteworthy of these works are: *The Moneychanger and his Wife* by Marinus van Reymerswaele, and *The Virgin and Child* by Quentin Metsys.

The *King's Room* or *Antechamber* houses a complete series of anonymous 17th-century paintings of Philip II's royal residences around

Chinese folding chair used by Philip II. German marquetry door in the Walkway. ▲

Sir Anthony More: Philip II. ▶

Madrid . They indicate the taste for architecture and passion for building that this monarch displayed when he was still prince. His greatest architectural achievement is undoubtedly the Monastery of El Escorial, of which some engravings by Pedro Perret, based on designs by Juan de Herrera, are also shown.

This series provides essential information about the building. The engravings hung here in Philip II's day, along with "still life paintings of many things found in our New World: some of the many different species of fowl... others of a great variety of large and small animals... and others of a thousand insects", a product of the great scientific work of Philip II's physician Francisco Hernández.

A corridor encircling the *King's staircase* leads to *Philip II's Bedchamber*, where he died on September l3th, 1598: "..in the same house and church of St Lawrence that he himself had built, ... almost above his own tomb, at five o'clock in the morning, when the dawn was breaking in the East ... and the seminary boys were singing the dawn mass, the last service held for his health, and the first for his salvation".

The position of the bed (inspired by his father's bed in Yuste) allowed the king to see, from his bedside, the countryside through two of the balconies and, on the other side, his Oratory and the Basilica's high altar. On the desk in the study, there is a "monstrance clock" made by Philip II's German clockmaker, Hans Evalo. Signed in 1583, this clock displays a typical mannerist design. The king used only the light of his little oil lamp when he wrote at night. In Philip's day the King's Bedchamber was decorated, among other works, with the *Seven Deadly Sins tabletop* by Bosch, now in the Prado. Among the paintings that now hang

▲ *King's Chamber.*

in the bedchamber are the *Sacra conversazione* by Benvenuto Tisi, *il Garofolo*; a *Pietà* by Gerard David and the *Portrait of Philip II as an Old Man* by Pantoja de la Cruz. The *ebony, silver and bronze altarpiece* beneath it is a Roman piece by Antonio Gentili based on a design by Giuliano della Porta, and was a gift from the Grand Duchess of Tuscany to the king in 1586. The rest of the paintings, all on religious themes, are Flemish and Italian and date from the early 16th century.

There are several precious objects worthy of note in the dresser: two *medieval chests*, one made of bone from the 10th century, and the other from the Limoges workshop dating from the 12th century; from the 16th century is the *Plateresque pyx* in the form of a temple by the famous goldsmith Luis del Castillo; and, from the end of the same century, two *paintings on agate* attributed to Annibale Carracci.

Top, the King's Chamber, with the Study and the Bedroom. At the far end, the oratory. Bottom, "Monstrance clock", ▲ *by Hans de Evalo, 1583.*

The austerity of these rooms is quite surprising given the royal pomp and splendour of the Modern Age and the fact that Philip II, king of Spain and the New World, was the most important European monarch of the century. Nonetheless, we should take into account that these "Royal Quarters" were located inside a Monastery in which Philip II, following the medieval tradition, used to live and cultivate his religious and filial piety.

After coming out of these rooms, we go along a corridor and down some stairs to the vestibule located between the Basilica and the Ante-Sacristy, from which we continue descending until we arrive at the *Pantheons*.

The Pantheons

ONE OF El Escorial's main purposes was to provide a burial place for the Spanish monarchs. Nevertheless, its founder's intention was not fully realised until after his death. According to some of the king's biographers, Philip claimed to have built a dwelling place for God and that his son, if he so wished, could build one for his bones, and for those of his parents. The two Pantheons reflect two distinct styles and centuries: the baroque style of the 17th century for the *kings and queens,* and an eclectic 19th-century style for their children, the *Infantes.*

The Pantheons are reached by a stairway leading off from the corridor linking the

▲ *The King's oratory, seen from the Basilica presbytery.*

Church and the Sacristy. The left-hand section leads to the Kings' Pantheon and the right-hand section to that of the Infantes.

The *Kings' Pantheon* is a dome-covered circular chamber whose circumference is divided into eight sections. Juan de Herrera conceived and built it in granite, but when Philip III decided to convert it into a Pantheon, he had the supervisor of the royal constructions, Giovanni Battista Crescenzi, dress it in marble and bronze, according to a project by Juan Gómez de Mora begun in 1617. Owing to various difficulties, the work continued throughout almost all of Philip IV's reign and was not completed until 1654.

Crescenzi, a Roman, directed the work done in bronze, carried out by Italian, in particular, Genoese craftsmen. Pedro de Lizargárate and Bartolomé Zumbigo the Elder were in charge of the marble work. It was during Philip IV's reign that the solution to the technical problems was found (a spring had appeared when the floor was lowered), along with the addition of grotesques to the dome, the new floor design and all the dressing of the stairway and entrances, the gilding of the bronzes and the addition of several more. The richness of the marble (the blue from Toledo and the red from Tortosa) and the bronze, the ornateness of the Corinthian order and the baroque exuberance of the grotesques

Left, door to the Kings' Pantheon. Right, Altar of the Kings' Pantheon. ▲

make this chamber a fine example of early Italian baroque that is more international than Spanish. Overlooking the altar is a *Christ on the Cross* by Domenico Guidi, a lesser known artist, but more fortunate than Gian Lorenzo Bernini and Pietro Tacca, who had previously produced other crucifixion scenes for the same altar that now hang in the school chapel and Sacristy vestry respectively.

The remains (after decomposing for years in an adjoining chamber known as the "Pudridero" or "Rotting Room") of the monarchs and wives who have been queen mothers rest in the urns, the kings on the right and the queens on the left of the altar, in chronological order from Charles I to Alfonso XIII, spanning a period of four centuries of the Spanish Monarchy. The only monarchs not buried here are Philip V and his son Philip VI, as well as their respective wives, given that they wished to be buried in the palaces they founded: La Granja de San Ildefonso and the Monastery of Las Salesas Reales in Madrid.

The *Infantes' Pantheon* was built on the orders of Isabella II, based on a project by José Segundo de Lema, and was completed in 1888. Each of the nine chambers, located beneath the Sacristy and the Chapter Houses, is overlooked by an altar and dressed in marble. The sculptures and adornments were produced in Carrara by Jacobo Baratta di Leopoldo and modelled on the work of the Aragonese sculptor Ponciano Ponzano. The style of this Pantheon, inspired by historical sources, gives rise to some new and truly funereal architectural forms. The appeal of the Pantheon lies in the cold richness of the stone, its historic interest and the 19th-century spirit that pervades it.

The *first chamber* is notable for its neoclassical altar with a *Descent from the Cross* by Carlo Veronese; the tomb of María Josefa de

▲ *Top, tomb of Don John of Austria, in the fifth chamber of the Infante's Pantheon. Bottom, detail of the vault of the Chapter Houses.*

◄ *On the previous page, general view of the Kings' Pantheon.*

Borbón, by Isidro González Velázquez; the tomb of the Infanta Luisa Carlota de Borbón, adorned with a statue of her granddaughter Isabella II, the queen who had this pantheon built; and the tomb of the Duke and Duchess of Monpensier and their daughters, by Aimé Millet. The *fifth chamber* contains the historicist tomb of Don John of Austria, fashioned by Giuseppe Galeotti according to a design by Ponzano. The *sixth chamber* is occupied by a mausoleum of Infantes who died before reaching puberty, and looks rather like a twenty-sided cake in white marble. The altar is adorned with a fine painting, *The Virgin of the*

Veil, by Lavinia Fontana (15890). The *ninth chamber* is of greatest historical interest as it contains sixteen tombs of members of the House of Austria.

At the far end of the Infantes' Pantheon are two vaulted cellars called the *platerías* or "silversmiths' cellars" from which a stairway leads up to the Chapter Houses.

The Chapter Houses

THESE LARGE and impressive Chapter Houses surrounded by a wooden bench were designed for the assemblies of the one hundred monks

Polygonal Mausoleum in the sixth chamber of the Infante's Pantheon. ▲

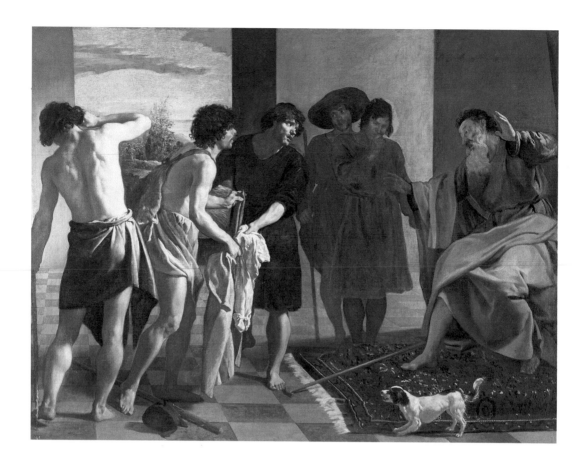

who lived in the Monastery. The two rooms are separated by a central entrance hallway. Their names, the *Vicarial Chapter House* and the *Prior's Chapter House*, are derived from the fact that they were presided over by the Vicar and Prior respectively. The last square-shaped room beneath the tower is the lower Priory Cell. These Chapter Houses, the Priory Cell and the entrance hallway form a magnificent row of four rooms, whose vaulted ceilings are painted with frescoes of grotesque motifs by Fabrizio Castello and Niccolò Granello. Most of the canvases that used to hang on their walls are now treasures of the Prado collection, though the remaining works are equally worthy of attention.

Titian's *St Jerome in Penitence* hangs in pride of place in the *Vicarial Chapter House*. Beside it

are two paintings of *vases of flowers* by Mario Nuzzi, called "dei fiori", and the two eremite saints, *St Paul and St Jerome,* by José de Ribera, who also painted the two magnificent canvases hanging on the long wall facing the windows: *St Francis Receiving the Stigmata* and *Jacob with Laban´s Flock.* One of Diego Velázquez's masterpieces, *Joseph's Bloody Coat Brought to Jacob*, painted during the artist's first sojourn in Rome, is also displayed in this room. Some of El Greco's most celebrated works hang between the windows, in particular *The Allegory of the Holy League* led by Philip II, the pope and Venice against the Turks in 1571.

The Prior's Chapter House is mainly decorated with Venetian art: Titian's *Prayer in the Garden*, which adorns the altar, as well as his

▲ *Diego Velázquez:* Joseph's Bloody Coat Brought to Jacob.

Rest on the Flight to Egypt and the *Last Supper*, which was unfortunately trimmed at the top to fit on the Monastery refectory wall; Tintoretto's *Esther before Ahasuerus* and *Christ and the Magdalene in the Pharisee's house;* Veronese's *Descent of Christ to Limbo* and Moretto da Brescia's *Eritrean Sybil* and *The Prophet Isaiah.*

The *lecterns* for reading the Epistle and the Gospel, fashioned by Juan Simon de Amberes in 1571, stand in the centre of the room. The *Priory Cell* still houses a collection of panel paintings by Hieronymous Bosch, known in Spain as "El Bosco", which include *The Way to Calvary, The Haywain* and *Christ Crowned with Thorns.* Above the altar is a *portable altarpiece belonging to Emperor Charles V*, a splendid piece made of gilded silver, enamel and wood fashioned by different workshops. The relief work and the apostles are more Italian, while the three embellishments are of a later, more international mannerist style.

The Main Cloister

THE MAIN Cloister galleries around the Courtyard of the Evangelists are decorated

▲ *Titian:* The Last Supper. *Below, José de Ribera:* St Francis of Assisi.

with fifty-four frescoes depicting the *Story of the Redemption* from the birth of the Virgin until the Last Judgement. They begin on the Processional Door, which links the Cloister to the Church. This series was painted by Pellegrino Tibaldi and his studio. The "seasons" in the corners are by Luis de Carvajal, Cincinnato, Tibaldi and Miguel Barroso.

The Main Staircase

THE MAIN staircase stands in the centre of the western gallery of the Cloister. This "most imposing and beautiful" staircase was not based on Juan Bautista de Toledo's designs; rather, it was apparently the work of Gian Battista Castello, known as "el Bergamasco". Added to its attractive architectural design is the lavishness of the ceiling frescoes painted in 1692 by Luca Giordano: *The Glory of the Spanish Monarchy* depicting Charles II in the centre of the western wall showing this apotheosis to his mother, Mariana of Austria, and his wife Mariana of Neuburg.

After admiring the staircase, it is worthwhile going for a stroll around the galleries and contemplating the paintings and the Shrine of the Evangelists. A number of important rooms are located around the Cloister, such as the *Old Church* and the *Sacristy*, but they are closed to the public.

The Courtyard of the Evangelists

THE COURTYARD of the Evangelists is one of the most interesting areas in the building from an architectural point of view, on account of the

▲ *Gallery of the main lower Cloister.*

Luca Giordano: The Glory of Spanish Monarchy *on the vault of the Main staircases.* ▶

façades that form the Cloister, based on a design by Juan Bautista de Toledo modified by Juan de Herrera, and the *Shrine* (the work of Herrera) that gives the courtyard its name.

In the centre of the garden, which is laid out in a typically cloistered style – in the shape of a cross – stands a Doric building that alludes both to the fountain of Grace and spiritual life (the Four Gospels), and also to the Garden of Eden with the four rivers that water all corners of the earth. The construction, the *Temple of the Evangelists*, was designed in 1586 by Juan de Herrera; the sculptures are by Juan Bautista Monegro.

The *Old* or *Provisional Church* served as a temporary place of worship for the monks from 1571 until the Basilica was completed in 1586. The three very impressive marble altarpieces are preserved in their original state. The largest one is adorned with one of Titian's masterpieces: the magnificent *Martyrdom of St Lawrence*. There are no words to describe the valour of this work; a similar one, albeit somewhat earlier, hangs in the church of the Gesuiti in Venice.

Despite being closed to the public, the vast rectangular *Sacristy* is worth mentioning for several reasons. Its ceiling is painted with grotesques by Granello and Castello. The paintings that once decorated its walls were among the Monastery's best, and some fine works of art still hang there to this day, such as Titian's *Christ on the Cross*, Ribera's *St Peter Freed by an Angel* and several canvases by Giordano. The finest example is the masterpiece painted by the leader of the Madrid school after Velázquez's death, Claudio Coello: the *Adoration of the Blessed Sacrament by Charles II*, in which baroque ingenuity extends into an imaginary space the perspective of the Sacristy as it appeared in the ceremony held in in this very room in October, 1684 – a true

snapshot of the Spanish Court. This painting has an anecdotal tale to tell as it also serves as a screen or veil that conceals the recess containing the Blessed Sacrament and reveals it only on special occasions. On such occasions the painting actually descends, sliding down on rails until it completely disappears from view, revealing the marvellous *Crucifixion* by Pietro Tacca and the Neo-gothic tabernacle that replaced the baroque one which disappeared during the Napoleonic invasion. The altarpiece and recess were based on a design by José del Olmo.

The Cloister leads out into the *Basilica Portico*, which gives access to the Basilica (p. 22) and *Kings' Courtyard*. The *Palace* or *Coach Courtyard*, where the entrance to the *Palace of the Bourbons* is located, can be reached by crossing the small yard (at the far end of the Portico on the left) or by going outside again and re-entering through the northern façade.

Claudio Coello: detail of The adoration of the Blessed Sacrament by Charles II. ▲

Shrine by Juan de Herrera, with sculptures by Juan Bautista Monegro, in the Courtyard of the Evangelists. ▶

The Palace of the Bourbons

GUIDED TOURS of the Palace are available by previous appointment on Friday afternoons and Saturdays. Appointments can by made by calling 91-890 59 02/5.

The Bourbon apartments occupy the eastern and northern sides of the Palace or Carriage Courtyard. During the rule of the Austrias, the inner bays looking out onto the Courtyard consisted of two enormous galleries; of the two external bays, the eastern one was occupied by the Royal Family, while the northern one was given over to rooms for the main courtiers. Charles III had all these spaces adapted to better accommodate the Royal Family, especially that of the Prince of Asturias, because like his predecessors, he lived in the "handle" part of the building's gridiron layout, which was also decorated according to Bourbon taste until the reign of Alfonso XIII. Nevertheless, when Charles IV came to the throne he did not wish to occupy the secular *King's Quarters*, and preferred to continue in the rooms to which he was accustomed. In order to give them a more dignified entrance, he had Villanova design a decorative staircase and completely modify the northern façade of the Monastery.

Its coherent decoration, the richness of the tapestries from the Royal Manufactory of Santa Barbara in Madrid and its relatively well preserved layout make it the most characteristic of all the Spanish Bourbon palaces.

Access to the Palace is via a *staircase* built by the architect Juan de Villanueva in 1793. From the upper landing, three passageways lead to the various apartments belonging to the members of the royal household. We will follow the route leading to the *King's Quarters*.

The three westernmost small rooms on the northern side were the *workshops of Charles IV*. These rooms contain several noteworthy religious paintings by Mariano Salvador Maella, as well as three bisque porcelain pieces from the Royal Manufactory at Naples, with portraits of the Royal Family. We next come to the *China Cabinet Room*, so-called after the neoclassical style cabinet displaying an English porcelain dinner service from the Copeland factory, a wedding gift from Britain's King George V to Alfonso XIII and Doña Victoria Eugenia.

The following rooms are decorated with tapestries from the Royal Manufactory of Santa Bárbara based on models, or "cartoons", painted by the artists whose names are displayed, and made to measure for the walls of this Palace and, in the majority of cases, for El Pardo. The tapestries thus completely cover the walls in order to protect the royal family from the cold, given that they inhabited El Escorial in autumn, and El Pardo in winter. Perhaps this desire to provide a cosy and warm environment partly explains the relatively small size of the rooms. Originally, the cartoons for each room were given to one artist and shared the same theme. This afforded the decoration a stylistic and thematic coherence that we have lost today, largely due to the many changes of place between the end of the 18th century and the beginning of the 19th century, which in the majority of cases must be respected.

The *Gala Dining Room*, formerly the Games Room, is decorated with tapestries made from cartoons by Goya, Bayeu and Castillo. The following room, which serves as a *vestibule* from the Villanueva staircase, has tapestries by Anglois, Antonio González Velázquez and Calleja imitating compositions by Teniers and Wouwerman. The Anteroom is adorned with

Madrid Royal Tapestry Manufactory: top, Ladies feeding the ducks, *according to a cartoon by José del Castillo.* ▲
King's oratory; below, the Walkway of the Statues in the Buen Retiro Garden, *according to a cartoon by Andrés de la Calleja.*
King's room, former Bedroom of the Infantas' chamber. Palace of the Bourbons.

▲ *Madrid Royal Tapestry Manufactory:* Ladies and noblemen strolling *(detail), according to a cartoon by José del Castillo. King's bedroom. Palace of the Bourbons.*

tapestries by Goya and Bayeu, and the Hall of Ambassadors contains tapestries by Bayeu. The *King's Oratory*, whose altar is adorned with a *Holy Family* by Luca Giordano, is located in a corner of the Palace Courtyard: the balconies of this row of rooms that look out onto the Courtyard are all south facing. The tour now continues along the west-facing façade.

The first four rooms belonged to the Infantas' Quarters. The first used to be the *Infantas' Playroom*, known today as the *Telemachus Room* after the "adventures of the young hero" depicted on the tapestries woven in Brussels by Leyniers. From here on all the tapestries are once again from the Royal Manufactory at Madrid. The following room was the *Bedchamber* and is adorned with tapestries woven from cartoons by Bayeu and Aguirre. The *Wet Nurses' Room*, known as the *Pompeian Drawing Room*, contains tapestries by Agustín and Juan Navarro. Tapestries designed by Goya, Castillo and Bayeu hang in the *Anteroom to the Infantas' Quarters*. The next two rooms belonged to the *Queen's Quarters*: the *Ushers' Room*, decorated with hunting scenes by Goya, Castillo and Aguirre; and the last in this row of rooms, the *Anteroom to the Queen's Quarters*, which leads directly to the Hall of Battles and is decorated with tapestries woven from compositions by Teniers.

All the following rooms look out onto the eastern façade, and from the Fine Woods Room onwards, to the north. The *Queen's Courtroom* is decorated with scenes by Bayeu, Goya and Castillo, among others; magnificently carved console tables dating from the time of Charles IV, and in the centre, an early 19th-century English piano by Thomas Tomkinson. This room leads into the Chapel, which contains candelabras and gilded silver accessories made by the Mártinez Royal Manufactory at Madrid. The *Everyday Dining*

Pompeian Drawing Room, Palace of the Bourbons. ▶

Room, formerly the *Boudoir*, has tapestries woven from cartoons by Goya, Aguirre and Castillo. The *Bedchamber*, now known as that of the king, contains a magnificent French bed which dates from the transition period between the neoclassical and Imperial styles and which belonged to Charles IV. The *Washroom* is decorated with scenes by Castillo and Aguirre, among others, Fernandine furniture and a curious structure that supports the toilet with neoclassical mural decoration.

The *Bedchamber*, now called the Queen's Bedroom, is adorned with tapestries woven from views of Madrid by Aguirre. The *Needlework Room* has tapestries with Pompeian motifs, woven from cartoons by Castillo to decorate this "oval room" which was occupied by the then Princess of Asturias, María Luisa de Parma, that still hang in their original position. The *Audience Room*, with scenes by Goya, Bayeu and Castillo, is furnished with a curious set of neo-Gothic furniture from the period of Ferdinand VII, made by cabinetmaker Angel Maeso in 1832.

Next are the so-called *Fine Wood Rooms*, which represent the extremely high international standards achieved in cabinet making and the decorative arts during the reign of Charles IV. The exotic wood marquetry in all four rooms (the *Study*, the *Oratory* and its *Anteroom* and the *Water Closet*) took from 1793 to 1831 to complete. The ornamental motifs are inspired by the classicist style, Pompeian forms and the style of Robert Adam and other late 18th-century European decorators. Diverse styles combine here in a rich and elaborate whole.

The Gardens

AFTER VISITING the building, it is worthwhile enjoying the gardens, and other outer

▲ *Top, Oratory. Below, King's Study. Fine Wood Rooms, 1793-1815. Palace of the Bourbons.*

Bedroom, called the King's Bedchamber, in the Palace of the Bourbons. ▶

features. Walking along the main façade, and descending the steps in La Lonja, we come to the gallery which links the Monastery and the Casa de la Compaña. Below the latter, a door leads across the Apothecary's Courtyard to the *Gallery of Convalescents* designed by Juan Bautista de Toledo, which has been described as a "fine piece of architecture and brickwork which forms two separate façades in these gardens" and whose arches do not form "a continuous row but have some spaces between them, giving it a charming appearance". As their name suggests, these "Sunny Walkways" were used by convalescing monks, as well as embellishing the retaining wall that encloses and links the different levels of the garden and La Lonja.

The Friars' Garden

THE FRIARS' Garden is located in the area resting on the sturdy walls that support the Monastery; the two parallel staircases lead down from it to the *orchard*, which is graced with a beautiful *pond* by Francisco de Mora.

When leaving the garden, it is worth going to the far end of pond wall in order to view the Monastery's *southern façade*. This path leads to the Casita de Arriba.

The Casita de Arriba or del Infante

THE SO-CALLED Casita de Arriba (literally Upper House) or Casita del Infante (Infante's House) was designed by Juan de Villanueva between 1771 and 1773 for the Infante

▲ *King's private garden and Prior's Tower.*

View of the rear façade of the Casita de Arriba or Casita del Infante and its gardens, to the south-west of the Monastery. ▶

Don Gabriel, the son of Charles III. Its noble Ionic architecture includes an Italian-styled terraced garden that offers one of the best views of the Monastery. It is open to the public during Holy Week and the summer months, except Mondays.

The ground plan of this pleasant recreational lodge, built around a two-storey high central hall, was originally designed for chamber music concerts, and is ultimately based on Palladian models. Typical of Villanueva is the entrance area with columns set in the walls.

Finally, walking down from the northern façade of the Monastery, through a fenced-off park, we come to the Casita de Abajo.

The Casita de Abajo or del Príncipe

THE CASITA de Abajo (Lower House) or Casita del Príncipe (Prince's House) was designed around the same time as the Casita del Infante for Don Gabriel's elder brother, the future Charles IV, by Juan de Villanueva. It was later enlarged between 1781 and 1784 by the same architect. As well as being larger, this House has an advantage over that of the Infante in that its interior decoration is in a much better condition.

The architectural design of the Casita del Príncipe (also seen in the Casita del Infante, but to a lesser extent) perfectly embodies the relationship between the main and secondary buildings and the layout of the gardens. The Casita's garden was also designed by Villanueva but was subsequently altered when conifers were planted there in the late 19th and early 20th centuries. Extensions were made to the *Large Drawing Room* and *Oval Room* in 1781, giving the ground plan a T-shape, and to the upper part of the western garden with the addition of the pond. The

"Pompeian" ceiling paintings on the ground floor are by Manuel Pérez, Felipe López, Juan Duque and Vicente Gómez. Most of the paintings representing religious, allegorical or mythological scenes are by the Neapolitan artists Luca Giordano and Corrado Giaquinto. There are a number of outstanding exquisite neoclassical pieces of furniture Such as the large Dining-room table, whose magnificent top inlaid with hard stones made by the Buen Retiro Royal Laboratory rests on Corinthian columns and dates from the reign of Charles IV.

From the garden of this Casita, the Basilica dome can be seen above the Park tree tops. It is 92 metres tall, 20 metres higher than the bell towers and 47 higher than the towers.

The Monastery has a total of 2,600 windows, 296 of which are outward facing, 1,200 doors, 86 staircases, 88 fountains, 16 courtyards, 15 cloisters and 9 towers, all within an area measuring 207 by 161 metres.

Vault of the central room of the Casita del Infante. ▲

Main facade and porch of the Casita de Abajo or Casita del Príncipe. ▶

Bibliography

HERRERA, Juan de: *Sumario y breve declaración de los diseños y estampas de la fábrica de San Lorenzo el Real del Escorial*, Madrid, 1589 (facsimile editions, 1954 and 1978).

SIGÜENZA, José de: *Fundación del Monasterio de El Escorial*. Books 3 and 4 of *Historia de la Orden de San Jerónimo* (Madrid, 1605)–, Ed. Turner, Madrid, 1986.

SANTOS, Francisco de los: *Descripción del Real Monasterio de San Lorenzo del Escorial, única maravilla del mundo*, Madrid, 1657.

XIMÉNEZ, Andrés: *Descripción del Real Monasterio de San Lorenzo del Escorial: Su magnífico templo, panteón y Palacio*, Madrid, 1764.

BERMEJO, Damián: *Descripción artística del Real Monasterio de San Lorenzo del Escorial y sus preciosidades después de la invasión de los franceses*, Madrid, 1820.

LLAGUNO Y AMIROLA, Eugenio: *Noticias de los arquitectos y arquitectura desde su restauración, por don Eugenio Llaguno y Amirola, ilustradas y acrecentadas con notas, adiciones y documentos por don Juan Agustín Ceán Bermúdez*, 4 volumes, Madrid, 1829.

QUEVEDO, José de: *Historia del Real Monasterio de San Lorenzo*, Madrid, 1849.

ROTONDO, Antonio: *Historia descriptiva, artística y pintoresca del Real Monasterio de San Lorenzo, vulgarmente llamado de El Escorial*, Madrid, 1863.

RUIZ DE ARCAUTE, Agustín: *Juan de Herrera, arquitecto de Felipe II*, Madrid, 1936.

HENERMANN, Theodor: "El Escorial en la crítica estético-literaria del extranjero, esbozo de una historia de su fama", in *El Escorial: Revista de cultura y letras*, 1943, pp. 319-341.

LÓPEZ SERRANO, Matilde: *Trazas de Juan de Herrera y sus seguidores para el Monasterio de El Escorial*, Madrid, 1944.

LORENTE JUNQUERA, Manuel: "La galería de convalecientes, obra de Juan de Herrera", in *Archivo Español de Arte*, 17, num. 63, 1944, pp. 137-147.

PORTABALES, Amancio: *Los verdaderos artífices de El Escorial y el estilo indebidamente llamado herreriano*, Madrid, 1945.

ZUAZO UGALDE, Secundino: *Los orígenes arquitectónicos del Real Monasterio de San Lorenzo del Escorial*, Madrid, 1948.

PORTABALES PICHEL, Amancio: *Maestros mayores, arquitectos y aparejadores de El Escorial*, Madrid, 1952.

ÁLVAREZ TURIENZO, Saturnino: *El Escorial en las letras españolas*, Madrid, 1963.

AA.VV.: *Monasterio de San Lorenzo el Real de El Escorial*. Patrimonio Nacional. El Escorial, 1964, 2 volumes.

CHUECA GOITIA, Fernando: *Casas Reales en Monasterios y Conventos españoles*, Madrid, R.A.H., 1966, Madrid, Xarait, 1982.

TAYLOR, René: "Architecture and magic: Considerations on the idea of the Escorial", in *Essays in the history of architecture in honor of Rudolf Wittkower*, Phaidon, London, 1967 (Spanish edition with revised and extended text: Ediciones Siruela, S.A., Madrid, 1992).

KUBLER, George: *Building the Escorial*, Princeton, 1982. Spanish ed., Alianza Editorial, Madrid, 1983.

OSTEN SACKEN, Cornelia Von der: *El Escorial, estudio iconológico*, Madrid, Xarait, 1984.

RIVERA BLANCO, Javier: *Juan Bautista de Toledo y Felipe II. La implantación del clasicismo en España*, Universidad de Valladolid, 1984.

AA.VV.: *El Escorial en la Biblioteca Nacional, Catálogo de la exposición, IV Centenario de la Fundación del Monasterio de El Escorial*, Madrid, 1985-1986. With an exhaustive bibliography of studies on the Monastery and travellers who mention it.

El Escorial: la Arquitectura del Monasterio, COAM. Madrid, 1986.

Catalogues of the exhibitions held to celebrate the IV centenary of the completion of the Monastery: *Las Colecciones del Rey. Las Casas Reales. Fe y Sabiduría. Iglesia y Monarquía*, Patrimonio Nacional; *Biografía de una época*, Ministerio de Cultura; *Fábricas y orden constructivo*, MOPU; *Ideas y diseño*, COAM; Madrid, 1986.

MOLEÓN, Pedro: *La arquitectura de Juan de Villanueva*, COAM, Madrid, 1988.

GARCÍA-FRÍAS CHECA, Carmen: *La pintura mural y de caballete en la Biblioteca del Real Monasterio de El Escorial*, Patrimonio Nacional, Madrid, 1991.

RUIZ GÓMEZ, Leticia: *Catálogo de Pintura Veneciana histórica en el Real Monasterio de El Escorial*, Patrimonio Nacional, Madrid, 1991.

CHECA CREMADES, Fernando: *Felipe II, mecenas de las artes*, Editorial Nerea. Madrid, 1992.

MULCAHY, Rosemarie: *The decoration of the Royal Basilica of El Escorial*, Cambridge University Press, 1994 (Spanish edition: "A la mayor gloria de Dios y el Rey": La decoración de la Real Basílica del Monasterio de El Escorial, Patrimonio Nacional, Madrid, 1992).

BUSTAMANTE, Agustín: "El Panteón del Escorial", Anuario del Departamento de Historia y Teoría del Arte, UAM, Madrid, 1992.

WILKINSON-ZERNER, Catherine: *Juan de Herrera, architect to Philip II of Spain*, Yale University Press, New Haven and London, 1993 (Spanish edition: *Juan de Herrera, arquitecto de Felipe II*, Ediciones Akal, S.A., Madrid, 1996).

BURY, John: *Juan de Herrera y El Escorial*, Patrimonio Nacional, Madrid, 1994.

BUSTAMANTE GARCÍA, Agustín: *La octava maravilla del mundo (Estudio histórico sobre El Escorial de Felipe II)*, Editorial Alpuerto, S.A., Madrid, 1994.

CANO DE GARDOQUI AND GARCÍA, José Luis: *La construcción del Monasterio de El Escorial. Historia de una empresa arquitectónica*, Universidad de Valladolid, Salamanca, 1994.

RODRÍGUEZ ROBLEDO, Piedad: *Pedro de Tolosa, primer aparejador de cantería de El Escorial*, Colegio Oficial de Aparejadores y Arquitectos Técnicos de Madrid, Madrid, 1994.

DI GIAMPAOLO, Mario, coord.: *Los frescos italianos de El Escorial*, Sociedad Editorial Electa España, Madrid, 1994.

BROWN, Jonathan: *El triunfo de la pintura*, Madrid, 1995.

Navarrete el Mudo, pintor de Felipe II. Exhibition catalogue, Logroño, 1995.

DI GIAMPAOLO, Mario, coord.: *Dibujos italianos para El Escorial*, Editorial Nerea, Madrid, 1995.

BROWN, Jonathan: *La Sala de Batallas de El Escorial: La obra de arte como artefacto cultural*, Universidad de Salamanca, Salamanca, 1998.

Felipe II, Príncipe del Renacimiento. Exhibition catalogue, Museo del Prado, Madrid, Sociedad Estatal para la Conmemoración de los Centenarios de Felipe II y Carlos V, 1998.

AA.VV.: *Felipe II y el arte de su tiempo*, Madrid, CSIC, 1998.

Reviews: *Reales Sitios* (Patrimonio Nacional), and *La Ciudad de Dios* (PP. Agustinos).

THE PRINTING OF THIS BOOK, PUBLISHED BY PATRIMONIO NACIONAL,
WAS COMPLETED ON 23TH JULY 2007, IN MADRID AT ARTES GRÁFICAS PALERMO, S.L